Epime(and Other 1 Berberidaceae

CW00828321

David G. Barker

Front cover and line drawings by Pam Ofield

Leaves, front cover, one-fifth size:

E. leptorrhizum	*Podophyllum peltatum*	*Jeffersonia diphylla*
E. dolichostemon	*E. × versicolor* 'Sulphureum'	*E. g.* 'Nanum'
E. acuminatum	*Bongardia chrysogonum*	*E. p.* 'Wisley'

ISBN 0 901687 13 8

Acknowledgements

I HOPE THAT THIS BOOKLET will be of interest to members, and I would like to begin by acknowledging the help which I have received from various people.

Professor W.T. Stearn has been very generous with his help and with copies of his recent articles in the *Kew Bulletin* and elsewhere. He has also kindly looked over the text despite his numerous commitments which include the preparation of his new Monograph on the genus. (His corrections and amendments have been incorporated.) Robin White, of Blackthorn Nursery, seemed an ideal person to ask about the latest introductions – of which there have been a number – especially after his superb exhibition of many of them at the RHS in 1995. Several of those he mentions, rare now, will become favourites in gardens in the not-too-distant future with his skill in propagation. Decie Needham, a member of the South Pennine Group of the HPS and of the Friends of the Botanical Garden, Sheffield, an enthusiastic admirer of epimediums, has researched the historical and medicinal details for her chapter on those aspects. Margaret Owen, holder of a National Reference Collection of *Epimedium* in Shropshire, and Elizabeth Strangman, of Washfield Nursery in Kent, have helped in showing me their collections and in talking about their plants. (There is also a National Reference collection at Wisley, in addition to the one that I hold.) Mihoko Watanabe, a Japanese horticulturist with whom I have corresponded, has given me information about those plants native to Japan. Herr Klaus Kaiser, of Coburg, Germany, has given me information about the use of epimediums there and my niece, Tina Wasmeier, has translated some of the text he sent.

Pam Ofield, who lives in Wiltshire, has made the fine drawings for the booklet and, what is more, has enjoyed doing them!

To all of these kind and busy people I am very grateful.

Introduction

I CAN THINK OF FEW GARDENS in which I have not seen epimediums – planted, I suppose, because they appealed to the person making the garden or with some definite purpose, such as ground cover, in mind. The fresh beauty of their young foliage entrances with its wide range of delicate greens, touched in a variety of ways with shades of red. It must be said that several epimediums do not have particularly striking flowers nor do they display their flowers at all well – they are predominately foliage plants. On the other hand, there are few garden plants which carry their flowers as elegantly as *E. davidii* does and in some, though relatively small, the blooms are wonderfully developed and complicated looking – those of *E. acuminatum*, for example, never fail to excite interest and amazement. The most gardenworthy forms are those carrying their large (or large clusters of) flowers above their evergreen foliage.

And then, of course, there is their good nature: few plants that we grow are as tolerant of almost all the various garden conditions found in Great Britain, though some are not happy on alkaline soils (which perhaps accounts for their absence from the catalogues of a number of nurseries in chalky areas and their less common culture in France). They also require no fuss nor special treatment though that is not to say that they will not repay some attention to their natural preferences.

Several of the other plants written about are less well-known and indeed some are rarely, if ever, seen in gardens. Some are uncommon in the wild and others are less tolerant of cultivation and none could really be described as showy in flower. They all, nevertheless, have their appeal and, given suitable conditions, make interesting and attractive garden plants. In the past few years I have found that the biggest problem in growing some of these plants has been drought. *Achlys, Caulophyllum, Diphylleia, Podophyllum* and *Ranzania* have all suffered – *Diphylleia* and *Podophyllum* quite quickly – from lack of rain. *Epimedium, Jeffersonia* and *Vancouveria* have been less affected but even some of these have shown distress. The least affected, perhaps, have been the Western epimediums and their hybrids, including most of the × *versicolor* cultivars and *Vancouveria hexandra*. What we need is the return of the good old English summer!

3

The Herbaceous *Berberidaceae*

THE BERBERIS FAMILY contains 15 genera and nearly 600 species of shrubs and herbaceous perennials. Shrubs include *Berberis, Mahonia;* × *Mahoberberis* and *Nandina.* Herbaceous members include *Achlys, Bongardia, Caulophyllum, Diphylleia, Epimedium, Gymnospermium, Jeffersonia, Leontice, Podophyllum, Ranzania* and *Vancouveria.* Of these, *Mahonia* and *Berberis* are similar, as are *Epimedium* and *Vancouveria, Diphylleia* and *Podophyllum,* and *Gymnospermium* and *Leontice* (these last two are united in *The RHS Plant Finder* under *Gymnospermium*). Apart from these pairs of close relatives, the genera in the family are rather dissimilar: they are linked by possessing a varied combination of common characters rather than by common possession of them all. They do nevertheless resemble each other more than they resemble plants of other families.

In consequence the genera have been variously arranged by botanists emphasising different characters. They have even been assigned to different families such as *Nandinaceae, Diphylleiaceae, Leonticaceae,* and *Berberidaceae* (in a narrow sense). Janchen in 1949, Meucham in 1993, Terabashi in 1985, Loconte in 1993 and Nickol in 1995 have all dealt with their classification but with different conclusions.

It seems reasonable, Professor Stearn suggests, to divide the Berberidaceae into three subfamilies:
* *Nandinoideae,* with only the very distinct shrub, *Nandina;*
* *Podophylloideae,* with *Podophyllum* and *Diphylleia;*
* *Berberidoideae,* with all the other genera – these in turn are divided into tribes such as:
    * *Leonticeae,* including *Caulophyllum, Leontice, Gymnospermium* and probably also *Bongardia*
    * *Berberideae (Mahonieae),* including two subtribes:
        * *Berberis, Mahonia* and *Ranzania*
        * *Epimedium, Vancouveria, Achlys, Jeffersonia* and possibly also *Bongardia.*

The placing of such remarkably distinct genera as *Bongardia* and *Ranzania* remains controversial. However, from the horticultural point of view, such disagreements have little importance. To a gardener the vegetative characters of *Ranzania japonica,* for example, appear rather similar to *Epimedium* and *Vancouveria* but its flowers are more like those of *Jeffersonia dubia.*

FAMILY FEATURES

Leaves spiral (opposite in *Podophyllum*), pinnate, ternate (divided into three more or less equal parts) or simple.

Flowers solitary or in panicles or racemes; bisexual and regular; most have parts in 3s, occasionally in 2s (as in *Epimedium*), always free from one another; never in 5s. Perianth usually in four whorls of three, the parts free from each other, but *Achlys* has no perianth parts, losing them early in flower development and in *Epimedium* there are three whorls of four – see below. Flower parts:

  • outer three (calyx) parts sepaloid – small and often caducous (i.e. falling off as the flower opens);

  • next three parts petaloid sepals and, in some, the showy part of the flower;

  • next three parts petaloid – these are missing in *Epimedium*;

  • inner three parts petaloid (usually nectary bearing and in *Epimedium* most have spurs).

Stamens – 6 usually (but 4 in *Epimedium* and up to 18 in *Podophyllum*); free; opposite the petals and usually the same number. Ovary – 1 carpel, with one to several ovules. Fruit – usually a berry; or a capsule, dry, dehiscent or not. Seeds – few or many; often with an aril, attractive to ants. They must all be sown fresh, otherwise germination is very erratic.

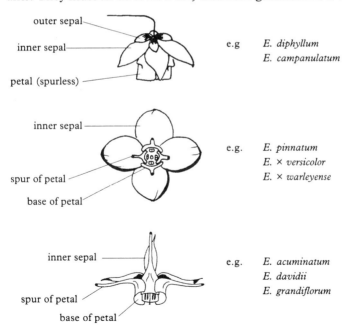

outer sepal

inner sepal

petal (spurless)

e.g   *E. diphyllum*
       E. campanulatum

inner sepal

spur of petal

base of petal

e.g.   *E. pinnatum*
       E. × *versicolor*
       E. × *warleyense*

inner sepal

spur of petal

base of petal

e.g.   *E. acuminatum*
       E. davidii
       E. grandiflorum

Range of flowers in *Epimedium*

Epimedium flower parts are in 4s; in the perianth the four parts of each whorl are arranged as 2 + 2. The perianth is in three whorls of four (or, perhaps more correctly, six of two) :

> • the outer, small, sepaloid, greenish, soon falling and called outer sepals.

> • the next petaloid and called inner sepals; coloured and conspicuous.

> • the innermost petals, size and shape vary according to species or cultivar and in many spurred and producing nectar (in the spurs in those with them); coloured.

They are protogynous flowers – the female parts mature before the male. When the anthers mature, the opening valves form a cover over the stigma and if cross-pollination has not taken place self-pollination can as the style lengthens to push the stigma among the anthers (but it produces no seed as they are self-sterile).

DISTRIBUTION OF THE HERBACEOUS MEMBERS

They are spread widely but not universally through northern temperate regions of the world – *Epimedium* and most of the others treated here are found in woodland in the wild. They are hardy in the range of temperatures normally experienced in those regions where they grow. The hardiness of some of the newest epimediums from China has not yet been tested in Great Britain. Those mentioned below are usually hardy in Great Britain, any exceptions being noted.

Bongardia, *Gymnospermium* and *Leontice*, tuberous genera dormant in the dry summers, are found in south-eastern Europe (though are very rare) and western Asia, growing on dry, stony hillsides or among shrubs. *Leontice* may be a weed of farmed ground, surviving cultivation by primitive tools as the tubers are 23-30cm(9-12in) below ground (modern methods reach deeper and they are now endangered). Adanson in 1763 and A.L. de Jussieu in 1789 were the first to associate *Leontice* with *Epimedium*; it must have been an imaginative step at the time since they are rather unlike.

The others are rhizomatous woodland plants showing disjunctive distribution (i.e. not continuously present throughout the range) but largely in eastern Asia and North America, the result of the last Ice Age. Then the area we know as Europe had extensive northern and southern ice sheets and lost most of its previous flora, sandwiched between the two. Eastern Asia had much less extensive ice sheets and in North America there was no barrier to migration (the plants could migrate back northwards as the ice sheet retreated). Except for *Bongardia*, *Gymnospermium*, *Leontice* and two *Epimedium* species, there are no herbaceous *Berberidaceae* endemic to Europe. *Caulophyllum*, *Diphylleia*, *Jeffersonia* and *Podophyllum* occur in both eastern North America and in eastern Asia. *Achlys* occurs in western North America and in eastern Asia. *Ranzania* is confined to Japan; *Vancouveria* to western North America; *Epimedium* to Eurasia, with the main centre of evolution in China.

ALPHABETICAL LIST OF GENERA

& MOST SPECIES, AND THEIR DISTRIBUTION

Achlys
A. californica - north-west North America.
A. triphylla – north-west North America.
A. japonica (*A. triphylla* subsp. *japonica*) – northern-central and northern Japan, Korea.

Bongardia
B. chrysogonum – western Asia, from Turkey to central Asia and Pakistan.

Caulophyllum
C. thalictroides – eastern North America, from New Brunswick to South Carolina and Tennessee.
C. robustum (*C. thalictroides* var. *robustum*) – Japan, eastern Siberia and China.

Diphylleia
D. cymosa – eastern USA, from Virginia to Georgia in the Appalachians.
D. grayi – coniferous forests in the mountains of northern Japan.
D. sinensis – central China.

Epimedium
Professor Stearn's current list; * marks species grown, not necessarily commonly, in gardens and listed in *The RHS Plant Finder*, along with varieties and cultivars
EE. acuminatum*, baicaliguizhouense, baojingense, brachyrrhizum, brevicornu, campanulatum, chlorandrum, coactum, davidii*, dolichostemon*, ecalcaratum, elongatum*, enshiense, epsteinii, fangii*, fargesii*, flavum, franchetii, glandulosopilosum, hunanense, latisepalum, leptorrhizum*, membranaceum*, ogisui, parviflorum, pauciflorum, platypetalum, pubescens, reticulatum, sagittatum*, simplicifolium, stellulatum*, sutchuenense, truncatum, wushanense and *zushanense* – China.
EE. alpinum* (the type species), *pinnatum**; *pubigerum** – Europe and western Asia.
EE. diphyllum*, grandiflorum*, sempervirens*, trifoliolatobinatum – Japan.

E. elatum – Kashmir.

E. macrosepalum – far eastern Russia.

E. perralderianum– north-western Africa.

Gymnospermium

Although *The RHS Plant Finder* includes *Leontice* with *Gymnospermium* in *Berberidaceae*, Professor Stearn keeps the genera separate and I shall do so here. Only *G. alberti* is listed as available in Great Britain and Eire. For details of the several rare species and subspecies and those described under *Leontice* see Rix and Phillips (1981) where they are put into *Podophyllaceae*. However, Rix later includes both of them in the *Berberidaceae* (Rix, 1982).

G. alberti (*Leontice alberti*) – central Asia.

Jeffersonia

J. diphylla – limestone woods in eastern North America, from Ontario and New York State to Wisconsin and south to Alabama.

J. dubia – Korea and eastern Manchuria, requires neutral or acid soil.

Leontice

L. leontopetalum – the arid fields and steppes in south-eastern Europe, north Africa and south-west Asia.

Podophyllum

P. hexandrum (*P. emodi*) – Afghanistan to central China.

P. peltatum – North America, from Quebec and Ontario to Florida and Texas.

P. pleianthum – central and south-eastern China and Tibet.

P. versipelle – central and western China and Tibet.

Ranzania

R. japonica – central Japan.

Vancouveria

VV. chrysantha, hexandra and ***planipetela*** (the three species) – occur from northern California to Washington state.

THE PLANTS

Culture Group: Group 1 – moisture-retentive, humus-rich soil in shade or semi-shade; Group 2 – more tolerant of drier soil, in sun or semi-shade.
Flowering times in Britain: winter (December, January, February); spring (March, April. May); summer (June, July, August); autumn (September, October, November).

TUBEROUS FORMS

Bongardia C.A. von Meyer, 1831.

B. chrysogonum (Linnaeus) Spach, 1839.

Commemorates A.G.H. von Bongard (1786-1839), a German botanist. Only the one species, from western Asia and possibly some Greek islands. Introduced into Britain in 1740.

Probably grown as much for its unusual and handsome leaves as for its transient flowers – pinnate leaves of sessile blue-green leaflets, usually 3-

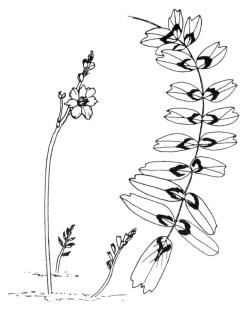

Bongardia chrysogonum

toothed at their tips, with red markings at their base. The leaves are 10-25cm(4-l0in) long and grow from the top of the tuberous rhizome, with their almost oblong leaflets paired or in a whorl of 3 or 4. The inflorescence, on a leafless stem, is a well-branched raceme to 60cm(24in) with yellow flowers 2-3cm(¾-1¼in) across. The sepals drop away as the flower opens and the 5-6 petals spread in a wide star, in mid-to-late spring.

Growing on stony hillsides and in dry cultivated ground, it requires a well-drained site where it gets a baking in its summer dormancy. I have made two attempts to grow it on a gravelly 'scree' but it stays only 2-3 years. It is probably better in a free-draining, not too rich mixture in a bulb frame or in a greenhouse pot, where I have it now and where dry summer conditions and winter wet may be better controlled.

Gymnospermium Spach, 1839.
The name means 'naked seed' and refers to the way the small capsule splits open before the seeds are ripe; they consequently ripen in a naked (i.e. uncovered) state.

9

Perhaps six small species, with tuberous rhizomes producing one basal and one stem leaf. Leaves lobed or ternate with leaflets sometimes lobed. Flowers in racemes with yellow petaloid sepals, often with red-brown veining, and reduced petals, in mid- and late spring. Most species found in dry places, scrub, rocky slopes and cultivated fields and require dry summer dormancy and little winter wet. Cultivate as for *Bongardia*.

G. alberti (*Leontice alberti*) (Regel) Takhtajan, 1970.
From central Asian mountains. The only one listed in *The RHS Plant Finder*.

The flowers begin to open as the crozier-shaped tips of the emerging stem straightens. The one stem leaf develops later; both it and the stem are reddish-brown at first, becoming green. The leaf is short-stalked with three main lobes, themselves divided with 4-5 unequal lobes, the largest lobe to 6cm(2¼in) long. The 5-15 flowers, in a crowded raceme, are up to 2cm(¾in) across and have six large petaloid sepals, yellow with reddish-brown lines from the outer base, thinning to about halfway; inside lined along their length. There are six very small petals, reduced to nectaries, and six stamens protruding from the little cup made by the petals. Height about 10cm(4in) at flowering, the flowers not opening flat but remaining somewhat cup-shaped; it increases to 20cm(8in) at fruiting. Flowers in the alpine house at Wisley in late February-early March. I grow it in an unheated greenhouse.

Leontice Linnaeus, 1753.
A contraction by him of the old name, *Leontopetalum*. A genus of three species in northern Africa, southern Europe and western Asia.

They have tubers, several much divided, somewhat leathery leaves on the stem and racemes of yellow flowers. The seeds develop in inflated, bladder-like fruit. Requires an open sunny situation in well-drained, gravelly loam.

Propagation – by seed, flowering may be a slow process. Seed germinates in autumn and makes a tiny tuber well below the soil surface (to 35cm/14in), where it remains. The two cotyledons emerge above ground in late spring. Use a deep pot for seeds and a gritty loam mixture in cold greenhouse or frame, always taking care with watering.

L. leontopetalum Linnaeus, 1753
The only species which has been introduced from the Mediterranean where it grows in arid fields, making large tubers perhaps 10-12cm(4-5in) across. Growing up to 50cm(20in) high with branched stems carrying much divided leaves, the lower with long petioles, the upper sessile, to 20cm(8in) long, with broadly ovate leaflets. The yellow flowers (1½cm/ ¾in across) are borne in several racemes, 5-15 flowers in each, in the axils of the upper leaves, forming a rounded head of flowers. The ovate fruits may be 2.5-4cm(1-1¾in) across.

RHIZOMATOUS FORMS

Achlys de Candolle, 1821.
Named after the goddess of obscurity according to the old RHS *Dictionary of Gardening* though it is not mentioned in *The New RHS Dictionary of Gardening* – perhaps it is too obscure!

A genus with three very similar species (or one species in three varieties), two in western North America and one in northern Japan, growing in moist woodlands, more or less shaded. The scaly thin rhizomes form open patches of plants with rather few leaves and, in my experience, they do not often produce flowers in cultivation, though I have seen them flowering, not profusely, in Washington and British Columbia.

Cultivation – Group 1, hardy, they will grow in deep shade, sharing it with ferns, mosses and perhaps trilliums.

Propagation – as in *Epimedium* (see page 22).

A. triphylla (Smith) de Candolle, 1821. (Deer-foot, vanilla leaf.)
North California to British Columbia, in coastal woodlands. It was brought to Britain in 1827.

The attractive deciduous leaves are very characteristic, divided into three thin, somewhat wedge-shaped leaflets, 5-10cm(2-4in) long and across at the widest part. They have more or less toothed, wavy edges, an apple-green colour, and are carried on long thin petioles, to about 30cm(12in) high. The flowers, without sepals or petals, have 6-15 stamens, white and clustered into a narrow spike 2.5-5cm(1-2in) long at first but lengthening and are rather insignificant. They are borne above the leaves, in late spring and early summer.

A. t. var. *japonica* (*A. t.* subsp. *japonica, A. japonica* Maximowicz) T. Itô, 1887.
Northern Japan and Korea. This species or variety differs in having only three shallow lobes to its leaves, and fewer stamens in its flower.

A. californica Fukuda & H. Baker
I have neither seen nor read about it.

Caulophyllum Michaux, 1603.
From the Greek meaning 'stem leaf', as the stem looks like a petiole. A genus of one species, with two varieties growing in shady, mountainous woodlands – one in eastern North America and one in East Asia.

The thin, 3-part compound, thalictrum-like leaf with about 15 oblanceolate leaflets, conspicuously veined, develops after the flowers and immediately below them. The small, star-shaped greenish-brown flowers are borne in a paniculate inflorescence; remarkably, the ovaries split open and the exposed fertilised ovules develop into blue, berry-like seeds, 1cm(½in) across.

Caulophyllum looks well with other woodland plants such as *Boykinia*, its relatives – *Diphylleia, Epimedium, Vancouveria hexandra* and *Jeffersonia* – and *Uvularia*. It also fits in with trilliums, lilies and ferns.

Cultivation – they are fully hardy and fall in Group 1. Grow in humus-rich, lime-free woodland soil, which retains moisture (they suffer in drought), preferably in deep shade.

Propagation – sow seed as soon as it is ripe, in a cold frame. Germination is likely to be both slow (perhaps a few years) and erratic, so that seedlings from the same batch of seeds may come up over 2-3 years. Divide in spring, just as growth begins, or after flowering. Very slow to increase.

Pests and diseases – the universal molluscs and vine weevil.

C. thalictroides (Linnaeus) Michaux, 1803. (Blue cohosh, papoose root.)

New Brunswick to South Carolina and Tennessee, coming to Britain about 1755. Leaves (sometimes only one) have three-lobed leaflets, to about 7 × 3cm(3 × 1¾in), from a thick rootstock. Insignificant flowers, about 1.2cm(½in) across, have, usually, six greenish-brown sepals, six petals (reduced to nectaries), and appear from mid- to late spring. Grows to 75cm(30in)and spreads to 18cm(7in).

C. t. var. robustum (Maximowicz) Regel

Eastern Siberia, Sakhalin, Japan, China, Tibet – the Asian variety, which is even less common than the type, has somewhat greenish-yellow flowers and is perhaps a little larger.

Diphylleia Michaux, 1803.

From the Greek meaning 'double leaf' – there are two leaves on the stem. There are three species which grow in moist humus-rich woodlands and by mountain streams.

The leaves are deeply bi-segmented, with toothed and pointed lobes. The leaves (like those of *Podophyllum*, emerging like little folded umbrellas) are peltate, large and handsome, on long petioles. The white, star-shaped, fragrant flowers with conspicuous yellow stamens, are borne in a terminal cyme, arising from between each pair of leaves, and quickly lose their petaloid sepals.

Cultivation – they are fully hardy and fall in Group 1. These handsome but uncommon foliage plants grow easily in moist leafy soil, in part-shade, appreciating wind shelter. They will be smaller in dry situations and have suffered in our droughts of recent years but with their roots in moist shade they can take more sun. They are ideal in woodland or a peat garden, with plants such as their near relatives *Podophyllum, Caulophyllum* and *Epimedium*. Rather later than might be expected in coming into growth in spring – I find I keep checking anxiously – they grow quickly when they do start.

Propagation – by division of the rhizome in spring or by seed sown fresh. Germination is erratic and slow and the seedlings may take several years to flower.

Pests and diseases – slugs and snails eat the resting buds and the young growth (a covering of fine chippings is a deterrent).

D. cymosa Michaux, 1814. (Umbrella leaf.)
From the Appalachian mountains from Virginia to Georgia, it was introduced into Britain in about 1812.

The stout rhizome produces upright stems; those which will flower have two leaves, 10-40cm(4-16in) across, almost cleft in two. Each of the two parts has several shallow, toothed and pointed lobes. Non-flowering stems bear a single larger leaf. The cymose inflorescence of white flowers, 2cm(¾in) across, may produce blue fruits and, as the stem becomes red, these make a striking contrast. Sometimes pubescent. Flowering in late spring-early summer it may reach to 1m(36in) and spread 30cm(12in).

D. grayi F. Schmidt
From Japan and Sakhalin and very similar to *D. cymosa* (see above) but smaller in almost every way, with fewer flowers, 1.5cm/½in across, and fruits with green stalks. Pubescent. It grows in moist humus-rich woodlands and by mountain streams.

D. sinensis Li
From central China but not known to me. Pubescent.

Epimedium
See pages 18-40.

Jeffersonia Barton, 1793. (Twin leaf.)
Named after Thomas Jefferson (1743-1826), third President of the USA. He was a noted gardener: 'No occupation is so delightful to me as the culture of the earth, no culture comparable to that of the garden.' (1811)

Two clump-forming species with basal leaves arising from fibrous roots; the long-petioled, glabrous leaves peltate, two-lobed and with toothed margins. The leaves enlarge and the petioles elongate after the flowers have fallen. Solitary, terminal, flat cup-shaped flowers have four green sepals, 5-8 lilac-blue or white petals, eight stamens and an oval ovary which forms a unique, somewhat pear-shaped fruit which opens just above its middle with a lip-surrounded mouth.

Cultivation – Group 1. These two hardy woodlanders enjoy moist, humus-rich soil in partial shade with a cooling mulch of good compost amongst their numerous thin stalks in late spring. They can be grown in the alpine house, needing cool shade for the summer. They associate well with other small woodland plants such as trilliums, disporums, smaller thalictrums, wood anemones and early 'bulbs' – snowdrops, erythroniums, corydalis but *J. dubia* might be overwhelmed by epimediums and vancouverias.

Propagation – by seed, sown fresh in a cold frame (a careful watch needs to be kept on the capsules as they ripen, turning yellow, for suddenly the seed is gone) or by division of the clump as growth begins in late winter or early spring (take care – the buds are brittle).

J. diphylla (Linnaeus) Persoon, 1805. (*Podophyllum diphyllum*)
From limestone woods in eastern North America, from Ontario and New York State to Wisconsin and south to Alabama. Introduced into Britain about 1792.

The larger of the two (height and spread to 30cm/12in), with leaves 10cm(4in) or so across, divided into two kidney-shaped, more-or-less toothed lobes, greyish-green and on a petiole 30-50om(12-20in) tall. The white flowers, 2.5-3cm(1-1¼in) across, usually with eight petals, which fall rather too soon, appear in late spring among the leaves. There is said to be a double form but I have not seen it though I would very much like to!

Jeffersonia dubia

J. dubia (Maximowicz) Baker and Moore, 1879. (*Plagiorhegma dubium* Maximowicz)
From Korea and eastern Manchuria. It has been in Britain since about 1918 (see above).

Smaller and even more beautiful in the early spring with its lilac-blue flowers which open before the leaves are fully developed and so stand above them. Gradually the flowers become more blue. They are 2-2.5cm(¾-1in) across, usually with six petals. The leaves are round to kidney-shape, bi-lobed (but not deeply so), glaucous green tinged violet (especially so at first). The clump grows to 20cm(8in) or so across and to 20cm(8in) tall. I also grow a white-flowered form but the blue remains one of my favourite flowers.

Note – *RHS Proceedings*, 1979. (Vol. civ., p3) re naming. *Plagiorhegma dubium*: Prof. Stearn said at a Committee meeting that the distinctions

14

were less than generic significance and both should be in *Jeffersonia*. In *Curtis's Botanical Magazine* 164 (1948) H.K. Airy Shaw expressed the opinion that 'the difference between *J. dubia* and *J. diphylla* are differences of degree rather than kind and therefore on a specific rather than a generic level.' Most botanists nowadays regard *Jeffersonia* and *Plagiorhegma* as forming one genus.

Podophyllum Linnaeus, 1753. (May apple.)
Rhizomatous perennials from China and the Himalayas and one from North America. The name comes from anapodophyllum, 'duck foot leaf', shortened by Linnaeus to podophyllum. There are two species of *Podophyllum* proper (having pink-white flowers) and about seven species of the Chinese Group *Dysosma* Woodson (with brown-purple flowers). For discussion of this and the five reasonably well-known species, which he lists under the name *Podophyllum*, see Rix (1982). He lists some twelve more, which are little known. I have kept to *Podophyllum* as listed in *The RHS Plant Finder*, though *P. pleianthum* and *P. versipelle*, both from China and both with nodding red-brown flowers hidden by leaves, are sometimes put into the *Dysosma* genus.

They have particularly handsome leaves, which emerge looking like tiny folded umbrellas, pushed up by the lengthening stem. The few, large leaves of a plant are radical, peltate or palmately lobed, with serrated or toothed margins. Some forms have leaves marked with purplish-brown patches between the conspicuous veining on the leaves and on the petiole – perhaps looking a little bit reptilian, rather like some arisaemas. The rhizomes, stems and leaves are very poisonous (though the powdered rhizome of *P. peltatum* has long been used as a purgative and an emetic like that of *P. hexandrum*) though the fruits are edible.

Hardiness – *P. pleianthum* and *P. versipelle* are not fully hardy. Rix states they are hardy at Kew, down to -10 °C(14 °F). They are likely to need winter protection if not in a very sheltered place. The others are hardy.

Cultivation – these are attractive foliage plants for woodland conditions (the flowers are few and rather hidden). Group 1: they are best in moist, humus-rich, leaf-mould soil in shade, or dappled shade. The North American *P. peltatum* is less demanding of moist soil and may spread more. All benefit from the use of good compost when planting. They need space for their spreading rhizomes but they never make really dense patches. Good among shrubs as well as with plants like anemones, epimediums and other of their larger relatives, and ferns. One should remember that they are poisonous. If you do have one with well-marked leaves, grow it where people may easily see it for they do attract attention!

Propagation – by seed, sown fresh and requiring stratification (germination is erratic but seedlings grow to flowering size quicker than most of their relatives) or by division of the extending rhizome system in

15

spring or late summer (or by removal of a piece of rooted rhizome).

Pests and diseases – slugs can cause much damage in the spring as the leaves emerge. I should think vine weevil might enjoy their rhizomes, but I have not found this or disease.

P. hexandrum Royle, 1834. (*P. emodi* Wallich ex Royle 1839. (Himalayan May apple.)

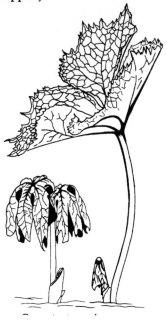

The young leaves of *Podophyllum hexandrum*

From the northern Indian Himalayas, east to China, it was brought to Britain in about 1845 (see facing page).

It grows to 45cm(18in) high by 30cm(12in). Wrinkled leaves to 25cm(10in) across and long, deeply lobed, toothed and with variable purplish-brown markings, long-stalked and radical, unfurling after flowering, two on each flowering stem. A few, solitary, flowers appear in late spring to midsummer, standing above the enlarging leaves, facing upward. They are open cup-shaped, 2.5-5cm(1-2in) across, with usually three sepals, six petals, white or pale pink, and 6 prominent yellow anthers. Large fleshy, red fruit, perhaps 5cm(2in) long, hang on the plant for weeks.

P. h.* var. *chinense Martyn Rix (1982) calls this 'a better garden plant'.

***P. h.* 'Majus'** Martyn Rix (1982) says this 'is reputed to be larger in all its parts.'
It appears that several other forms have been described fairly recently.

P. peltatum L. 1753. (American mandrake; May apple; wild jalap.)
Eastern North America, from Quebec to Texas and Florida. Known in
Britain since about 1664.
  It grows to 45cm(18in) tall; its spread is variable. Creeping patch-
forming, with glossy, peltate, deeply 3-9 lobed radical leaves on long stalks,
well developed at flowering, to 30cm(12in) across and long. Flowering
stems have two leaves; non-flowering only one. Semi-nodding, solitary,
open cup-shaped flowers, about 5cm(2in) across, are borne rather hidden
beneath the leaves. The flowers open in mid-spring to early summer and
have waxy-white to pale pink petals (usually nine) and nine stamens. They
are followed by yellowish-green apple-like fruit, 2.5-5cm(1-2in) long.

P. pleianthum Hance, 1883. (Chinese May apple.)
From Taiwan, central and south-eastern China, it was introduced into
Britain from the Hong Kong Botanic Garden in 1885.
  It grows to 75cm(30in) high and 45cm(18in) wide. The short rhizome
forms large, peltate leaves to 30cm(12in) across and long, with shallow,
finely-toothed lobes, conspicuous veins and a glossy upper surface. Small
clusters of 5-8 deep crimson-purple flowers, with 6-9 petals to
6cm(2½in) long, hang under the leaves, not opening very wide, in early
to mid-spring. The fruits are dark red.

P. versipelle Hance, 1883.
From western China, it probably came to Britain in 1903.
  Similar to *P. pleianthum* but smaller in all parts. The more deeply-lobed
paler green leaves are about 15cm(6in) across and the flowers have deep
brownish-crimson petals 2-3.5cm(¾-1½in) long. They hang in clusters
of up to 15 between and below the leaves in early summer and are
followed by red fruits.

Ranzania T. Itô, 1888.
Named after the eighteenth-century Japanese botanist Ono Ranzan
(1729-1810), the 'Japanese Linnaeus', this monotypic genus is a beauty
but a great rarity. A small rhizomatous plant from the deciduous
woodlands of northern Honshu, Japan, it enjoys similar conditions to its
relatives, growing with *Caulophyllum*.
  The smooth stems each bear two (usually), opposite, 3-part leaves at
their apex but before these develop fully, the flowers open from between
them. They number 1-6 and are pendulous on long (4-8cm/1½-3in)
pedicels, in a loose terminal group; the stem becomes upright in fruit,
which is an elliptical white berry when ripe.

R. japonica T. Itô, 1888. (*Podophyllum japonicum*)
It grows to a height of 10-15cm(4-6in) in flower, later to 30-40cm(12-
16in) and spreads to 20cm(8in). The tri-lobed leaflets are orbicular and
cordate at their base, bluish underneath and 8-12cm(3-5in) across. The
star- or shallow cup-shaped, pale lavender-violet flowers are somewhat

similar to those of *J. dubia*. They are 2.5cm(1in) across, with six petaloid sepals, 1.5cm(1¾in) long and 3-4 times larger than the six small, nectary-bearing petals, and six stamens. Mid-to-late spring.

Cultivation – hardy (at least to -10 °C) though damaged by late frost and requiring a moist, shady position in a cool, leaf-mould rich soil. A Group 1 plant for light woodland, to grow with *Disporum, Caulophyllum,* and *Jeffersonia,* though perhaps (because it is rather similar vegetatively and less vigorous) away from *Epimedium.* It resents disturbance.

Propagation – by division in spring or by ripe seed, covered with a thin layer of fine grit in a cold frame. Takes 18 months to germinate and about 3-5 years to flower.

Pests and diseases – not known. Slug damage likely in spring and it seems a likely candidate for vine weevil damage.

Vancouveria C.F.A.Morren and Decaisne, 1834.

It is a genus with three species (the North American equivalent of *Epimedium*), named after Captain George Vancouver (1757-98) of HMS *Discovery,* who explored the north-west coast of North America.

Hardy, woodland plants, spreading, with   slender, horizontal, rhizomes. It is useful groundcover in cool leaf-mould rich soils in sunny or partially-shaded areas of woodland, and also happy (at least *VV. hexandra* and *planipetala* are) in lightly shaded coniferous plantations.

They are similar to *Epimedium* but smaller and with six (not four) inner sepals, petals and stamens. Leaves radical, divided, usually into nine rounded but somewhat tri-lobed leaflets, cordate at their base. Two species are evergreen with slightly leathery, glossy, dark green foliage. The wiry flowering stems, usually without leaves, hold the inflorescence of a few pendulous small flowers in a panicle above the foliage. The flowers have three smaller deciduous outer sepals, and six reflexed larger inner sepals, six reflexed petals with apical nectaries and six stamens. The fruit is a capsule which splits lengthwise to release the smooth black seeds.

Hardiness – *V. hexandra* appears to be hardy down to -15 °C(5 °F); the other two to -10 °C(14 °F) and, if there is no snow, they would be safer with some cover such as leaf-mould.

Cultivation – Group 1 (preferably) or 2 if not too exposed. As for *Epimedium.*

Pests and diseases – slugs and snails eat the young growth and probably deer and rabbit would too. Vine weevil.

Propagation – as for *Epimedium.*

V. chrysantha Greene, 1885.

Native to south-west Oregon and northern California, it is rather more drought resistant than the other two, growing in scrub on hillsides, rather than in woodland. Introduced into Britain in about 1935.

Slowly spreading, forming open patches of purple-tinted, dark green, glossy evergreen leaves, divided into firm leaflets (nine – though sometimes three or five). These have thickened edges and are about 3.5cm(1½in) across. In late spring and early summer, small (1.2cm/½in across) golden yellow flowers are carried to 20-30cm(8-12in).

V. hexandra (Hooker) C.F.A.Morren and Decaisne, 1834.
North Washington to central California, it usually grows in redwood or pine forests. Date of its introduction into Britain not known, except that it was in the late years of the last century. It is the one most like an epimedium.

Deciduous (though often hanging on into the New Year), bright green leaves, 2-3 ternate with three or five leaflets, which are thin, ovate and to about 7cm(3in) across. In late spring and early sumner, white flowers, l-1.3cm(½in) long and 1.8mm(¾in) across, are carried 20-80cm(4-16in) high. I find this the most vigorous and spreading species, covering some 1.5m(5ft) square in a few years. The most hardy to -15 °C(5 °F).

V. planipetala Calloni, 1887.
South-west Oregon to central California, growing in coastal redwood woodland. Probably brought to Britain about 1909.

Gently spreading – I find it the slowest of the three, and the shyest to flower. Leaves 2-3 ternate and thick, leathery leaflets, to 5cm(2in) across, with thickened, usually wavy margins. They are evergreen and a glossy, dark green. In late spring and early summer white flowers, some with lavender shading and about 6mm(¼in) across and long, are borne up to 45cm(18in) high. The least hardy – perhaps to -10 °C(14 °F).

Epimedium – history and medicinal uses

V. D. NEEDHAM

THE NAME 'epimedium' (*epi* = upon; Media = the country of the Medes, south-west of the Caspian Sea), was first used by the Greek herbalist Pedanios Dioscorides of Anazarba (or Anazarbos), near Tarsus in Cilicia, in the first century AD. He described a plant with ivy-like leaves and a black root, growing in watery places, with no flower or seed, which bears no relationship to the European *E. alpinum*. Theophrastus (*c.* 371-287 BC, a disciple of Aristotle who took over his garden in Athens) mentions an 'Epimenides squill' in his *Enquiry into Plants*, the earliest surviving Greek herbal. The Roman, Pliny the Elder, who later used Theophrastus's work, employed the word 'Epimenidium'. This may have been derived from the name of the poet and prophet Epimenides, who lived in the sixth century BC in Knossós, Crete, and who dabbled in magic. Pliny states that the herb had the properties of 'thickening and cooling' and was to be avoided by women.

John Gerard,1545-1612 (*The Herbal or Generall Historie of Plantes*, 1597), says that he received his plant from the French King Henri IV's herbalist, Jean Robin, and that he 'thought it good to call it Barrenwoort in English; not because that Dioscorides saith it is barren both of floures and seeds, but because (as some authors affirme) being drunke it is an enemie to conception'. He, however, affirmed that it had no virtues as yet 'in physicke'. The woodcut used to illustrate *E. alpinum* (named by Linnaeus in 1753) was that of Tabernaemontanus (*Eicones plantarum*, 1590), who worked in Frankfurt-am-Main. This later was replaced by the less accurate one of de l'Obel, used by Parkinson and others.

John Parkinson, 1567-1650, apothecary and herbalist to James I, published his *Theatrum Botanicum* in 1640, drawing on the unpublished botanical notes of Mathias de L'Obel (or de Lobel). L'Obel was a French herbalist (1538-1616), in charge of Lord Zouche's botanical garden at Hackney, when he also made a survey of the British flora. Parkinson said of *E. alpinum* that its special virtue was 'to keepe womens breasts from growing over great, being made into a cataphasme, with oyle and applyed thereto; ... the roote would make women barren that took it inwardly, as also the leaves made into powther and taken in wine'.

Linnaeus received *E. alpinum* from Empress Catherine the Great of Russia and it was grown in his 'Siberian garden' at Hammarby (about seven miles from Uppsala) and at Clifford's Garden at Hartecamp, Holland. Linnaeus was at the latter for two years, as physician to George Clifford and looking after his herbarium and garden – 'one of the finest in the world' according to Linnaeus. He described the plants in the garden and greenhouses, including exotic rarities such as cocoa, coffee and tea plants, in *Hortus Cliffortianus* which was published in 1737, the same year as his more famous *Genera Plantarum*.

The oriental species have been used medicinally for centuries and have many folk names. Pin Yin has two terms for *Epimedium: Yinyanghuo**, meaning 'licentious or lascivious goat herb' and *Xianlingpi*, meaning 'active spleen'. The dried leaves of *EE. acuminatum, grandiflorum* and *sagittatum* were used for a tonic. Other descriptive names for *E. grandiflorum* are *Shilingpi* ('first efficacious spleen'); *Qianliangjin* ('thousand ounces of gold'); *Sanzhijiuyecao* ('three branches, nine leaves herb') and *Fangzhangcao* ('give up stick herb' – apparently the drug gave a man over fifty the strength to discard the stick he was entitled to use!). *Epimedium sagittatum* was known as *Jiaoyanyzazo*, 'the horny goat weed'.

The Japanese name for *E. grandiflorum* is *ikari-sô* or *ikari-gusa* (*ikari* = anchor; *sô* or *gusa* = plant, referring to the four-clawed anchor used by Japanese fishing boats, which resembles the flowers' long-spurred petals).

The leaves of *E. grandiflorum* on analysis were found to contain a glycoside (icarin or epimedin) and an alkaloid. An extract of the leaves, taken orally, increased the frequency of copulation in animals tested and intravenous injections of the glycoside increased the seminal fluid in dogs. It is used as an aphrodisiac. *Epimedium acuminatum* was found to contain hexacosyl alcohol; hentriacontane; oleic, linoleic, palmitic and stearic acids and phytosterol. It stimulates the secretion of hormones and is used to treat impotence and forgetfulness. It is also recorded as anti-asthmatic, anti-rheumatic, antitusive and an aphrodisiac and is used in treating renitis (a kidney disease) and eye ailments.

The Chinese use *E. sagittatum* as a tonic for kidney yang deficiency and liver ailments. It eliminates 'wind-damp' ailments such as rheumatism, lumbago, cold hands and feet, spasmus (involuntary muscle contraction) and numbness. Again it is used as an aphrodisiac and in treatment for impotence, premature ejaculation and spermatorrhoea. The drug is said to dilate the capillaries and larger blood vessels and lower the blood pressure. It remedies absent-mindedness by flooding the brain with blood. It is a common ingredient in 'spring wine' (which is possibly a tonic or an aphrodisiac in folk treatment). Other uses include treating corneal infections and ulceration of the eye. It is used to treat sterility and barrenness in women – the opposite of the use recommended in Gerard's *Herbal*. It is mentioned in Chinese herbals as an aphrodisiac for sheep!

Epimedium species are used in treating breast cancer and other tumours and, in the last 30 or so years, Chinese medical records report three patients cured of uterine cancer. Chinese medical herbals list its use as an analeptic (stimulates breathing), carminative (sedative), sudorific and for treatment for weak knees and neurasthenia (nervous exhaustion)!

* *Yinyanghuo* appeared in the ancient Chinese herbal, Emperor Shen Nong's *Canon of Materia Medica* (*Shen Nong Bencaojing* – 'the divine farmer' – is a charming description of a plantsman).

Epimedium

(Barrenwort, Bishop's hat.) Elfenblume in Germany. E.A. Bowles described them very aptly as 'happy mediums'.

A genus of 46 named species (according to Professor Stearn, August 1996) though there are more to be described and named, and possibly more to be found. Professor Stearn is the world authority on *Epimedium* (he has named nine of the species) and his new monograph will incorporate discoveries by plant collectors, such as Martyn Rix, Roy Lancaster and especially the Japanese authority Mikinori Ogisu, who have introduced several species from China in recent years. Some of these were seen at the RHS in the splendid display mounted by Robin White of Blackthorn Nursery in the spring of 1995. The older hybrids and cultivars are better known in gardens than are the majority of the species and new plants are still coming from the Far Fast, especially species from China and cultivars from Japan. It is to be hoped that the Japanese do not name too many, not very distinct plants. It seems a forlorn hope: Professor Stearn tells me that they have already named at least 160 cultivars!

Epimediums are native to two main areas of the northern hemisphere:

(i) south-east Europe, Algeria and Asia Minor – four species grow in light woodland and scrub and shady rocky places.

(ii) temperate east Asia – thirty-three species are named from China (at least 20 are recorded from Sichuan where the isolated valleys provide ideal conditions for speciation); four from Japan (one of these also in Korea and Manchuria), and one from Kashmir. The Asian species grow in similar situations to those of the first group though require more shade and moisture.

They are clump-forming, having thin, compact or spreading rhizomes, producing mainly basal, compound leaves, long-petioled and thin but often leathery. These have 3-9, or more, ovate/lanceolate/acuminate/acute/more or less arrow-shaped leaflets. These are unequally cordate (lobed) at the base, and with more or less spiny margins. Most have a leaf on the flowering stem (the Chinese species usually have two); the two African-Caucasian species, *E. pinnatum* and *E. perralderianum*, are the only ones always to have leafless flower stems. Some are deciduous in autumn but others only after the new leaves appear, giving attractive evergreen winter clumps.

Small, pendulous, more or less cup-shaped or saucer-shaped flowers, perhaps 4-12 or 10-50 depending on the species, in yellow, red or purple shades, or white, are borne in loose racemes or panicles in mid-to-late spring and one, *E. membranaceum*, regularly into summer. The flower parts are in fours and the outer perianth parts (outer sepals) – two slightly smaller than the other two – fall away as they open. The inner sepals are usually larger and conspicuous – like petals to most of us. Many have spurs developed from their petals and though some have very small spurs remaining beneath the inner sepals in others the spurs are larger and held outwards so that the flowers resemble small aquilegias or spiders – though with only four 'legs'! Four species have flat spurless petals, thought to be the most primitive arrangement.

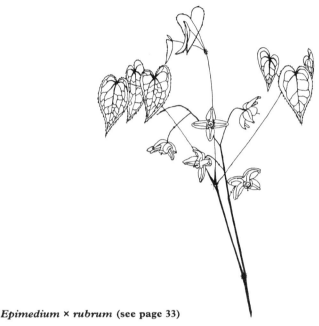

Epimedium × rubrum (see page 33)

The nectar produced by the flowers is attractive to bees of all sorts. Both flowers and foliage are good for cutting and may be dried by hanging them in a dry airy place. The leathery leaves are usually attractively red or coppery-brown tinted or marked in the spring. Some colour to russet-brown shades in the autumn as well. The more robust epimediums make excellent ground cover under trees and among shrubs, as well as in a border, and provide an early show of foliage and flowers before most herbaceous perennials are far advanced.

Hardiness – most are fully hardy, though late frost and cold winds may damage young foliage and flowers (especially in some of the Chinese species). These Chinese forms may require some cover if winter temperatures below -10 °C(14 °F) are prolonged and are best in places away from both wind and the hottest sun, sheltered perhaps by shrubs or trees. More foliage will replace that damaged by frost, though new flowers may not develop – this happened to my *E. acuminatum* a few springs ago but it recovered. Some of the most recent introductions have not yet really been tested for hardiness.

Cultivation – most are tolerant of widely differing conditions, though the Japanese species are not happy on alkaine soils. (In *The RHS Plant Finder*, one nursery, specialising in plants for alkaine soils, no longer lists any and another on chalky soil only supplies *E. grandiflorum* and *E.* × *youngianum* 'Niveum'.) All are best in humus-rich, moderately moist, though well-drained soils. Some – best are the strong-growers – tolerate dry shade but fewer flowers develop. On a moister soil they will take more sun. Occurring naturally in the light shade of deciduous woodland, they may be grouped according to their main requirements – though most will grow quite well under either set of conditions, given good drainage:

Group 1 – moisture-retentive, humus-rich soil in shade or semi-shade – those from Asia.

Group 2 – more tolerant of drier soil, in sun or semi-shade – those from the Mediterranean and the Caucasus.

In the droughts of 1994-5 some showed more distress than others. The worst affected in my garden were *E. grandiflorum* and its cultivars 'Rose Queen' and 'White Queen'; × *versicolor* 'Cupreum'; × *youngianum* 'Lilacinum', 'Niveum' and 'Roseum' (the × *youngianum* cultivars do prefer a moister situation than most).

In most years, I think it better to clip off leaves of the 'evergreen' types in late winter or early spring so that new growth and flowers may be better seen but this is an area of debate and personal preference. It does mean losing the colour which the older leaves provide, whether it be the green of some or the russet browns of others. Many are splendid winter-foliage plants though in some cases the evergreen leaves become brown and battered (to an extent dependant upon the weather) so that enjoyment of them varies with people's untidiness tolerance. The young leaves, and the flowers, grow up through the old and can be seen quite well in most as the old foliage tends to flatten outwards from the clump at this stage. I compromise: where there is good colour and the old leaves are not too tatty I leave them on or remove just the worst and the outer ones. The timing of leaf removal depends to some extent on the weather, for the young growth is susceptible to frost and cold winds. However, if it can be done before young growth is much advanced, it can be done more easily – cutting the clusters off with shears rather than separately with secateurs, without breaking tender shoots. The clumps look very bare for a time and are, of course, more exposed to frost and cold winds than they would have been had the old leaves been left but the new foliage is lovely, right from its first tiny tender growth through the gradual enlargement of the leaflets to its apple green and often coppery-red shaded full size. The unbending croziers of flowers are very attractive too.

Good preparation of their site, with leaf-mould and compost, plus bonemeal, is preferable and an annual spring mulch of good compost with some bonemeal and perhaps a little Growmore, or similar general fertilizer, helps maintain vigour. Some form close clumps, making a lovely mound; others, with longer, thinner rhizomes spread more, but not too invasively, making wider, looser clumps – a drift, if you like. Their dense network of fibrous roots will in time remove soil nutrients and leaf size and the numbers of flowers will decrease. Those forming tight clumps in particular need to be taken up in the autumn every 3-5 years, divided and replanted in a new place or into revitalised soil. The more spreading sorts need less frequent replanting. Plant the smaller and the clump-forming sorts some 35-45cm(14-18in) apart and those with more creeping rhizomes 45-60cm(18-24in) apart.

Propagation – by division as growth begins in early spring or in early autumn when leaves are mature – the latter is probably the better time, as new roots will grow vigorously then if there is no prolonged drought, and the young spring growths are brittle and easily snap off. Washing off soil from the roots makes it easier to see where to cut. Two forks back to back usually work if the clump isn't too old (the older rhizomes become very tough) though a sharp knife may be necessary to cut through the hard woody base or even a chop from a spade. Each division should have some foliage on it but cut away any that is damaged and, if there is much, remove some leaves to reduce transpiration. Keep watered until established. Alternatively, separate rhizomes in winter and pot up for new plants by the spring or scrape away soil from the plant to take rhizome cuttings in winter, root under glass and plant out after danger from frost has passed. Generally more care is needed with the Chinese species when dividing the clump, as they seem to dislike disturbance more.

By seed, sown fresh in late summer; you need to keep an eye on the developing fruit as they open and lose their seed while they and it are still green or yellowish. The seed should be sown straight away and kept in a cold-frame over winter. It should germinate in the spring. In nature, hybridisation may not be common because of isolation but it can occur (more so, apparently, in Japan than in China). In cultivation hybridisation occurs if species are grown together and Elizabeth Strangman at Washfield Nursery and Robin White at Blackthorn Nursery are producing some fine seedlings from crosses involving some of the newer introductions.

Pests and Diseases – generally free from problems, though mosaic virus may cause stunted growth and spotted leaves and victims are best destroyed. Vine weevil grubs are the worst pest – always thoroughly wash the roots of any acquired plants. Slugs, snails and some small rodents eat the young growth and other herbivores, like rabbits and deer, can be a nuisance – gardeners devise their own methods of defence or attack. Aphids may feed on young leaves and cause them to become distorted.

EPIMEDIUMS - ALPHABETICAL LIST

Deciduous unless stated differently. Measurements vary (height and spread vary with soil and situation); the figures given refer in almost all cases to plants grown in my garden, which is rather a dry one.

E. acuminatum Franchet, 1886.

From western and central China. First found by the French missionary, Perny, in 1858, it was introduced to Britain in the early 1980s by Mikinori Ogisu, Roy Lancaster (from Emei Shan) and others.

Epimedium acuminatum

Clump-forming (30 × 45cm/12 × 18in), with evergreen leathery leaves divided into two trifoliate parts. The leaflets (8.5-17 × 3-6cm/ 3¼-7 × 1¼-2½in) are ovate-lanceolate, the lower two of each part with very unequally-lobed bases; they have bristly margins and long, pointed tips. Young leaves are pale green, marked with reddish brown and mauve; they become darker green and glaucous, almost metallic, beneath. Flowers, rose-purple and white, 3-4cm(1¼-1½in) across. The petal is shaped like a cornucopia, dusky purple at the mouth, with a long (3cm/1¼in) curved spur, shading to white at the tip. They are borne in mid- and late spring to early summer on a flower stalk which bears a leaf. Stamens have green filaments and anthers.

Cultivation – Group 1.

26

E. alpinum Linnaeus, 1753. (Barrenwort.)
The 'little, dingy *E. alpinum*, known only in the gardens of botanists ...'
(Lindley; *Botanical Register*, vol. 22, 1849) is perhaps too denigrating, for
it is a useful, very tolerant, almost indestructible plant.
From southern Europe, along the southern parts of the Alps in Italy and
east into the former Yugoslavia and Albania, in mountainous woodland.
Decie Needham, author of the historical and medicinal section of this
booklet, found a references to it in Sowerby's *English Botany*, 1798, on
Carrick Fell, Cumbria. It was also said to be collected in Bingley Woods,
Yorkshire, though there is a hand-written note, dated 1797, in the Suffolk
County Record Office, Bury St Edmunds, which expresses doubt about
this. It has apparently been known in Britain since 1597, so these 'wild'
plants were garden escapees as it is not thought to be endemic.
Height 15-30cm(6-12in), spread 30cm(12in). Biternate evergreen
leaves with 5-10 cordate, spiny-margined leaflets, 5-9 × 3.5-7cm(2-3½ ×
1½-3in), often colouring crimson in autumn before dying. Almost
spurless and not particularly showy small flowers, 1-1.2cm(¼-½in)
across, with red sepals and yellow petals, are soon over-topped by the leaf
on the flower stalk.
Cultivation – Group 2.

E. × cantabrigiense Stearn, 1979.
The cross, *E. pubigerum × E. alpinum*, occurred in the 'wilderness' garden
at St John's College, Cambridge, some time during the Second World
War and was named in 1979 by Professor Stearn (*The Plantsman*, Vol.1,
pt.3, Dec. 1979). (This is also interesting as it includes a technical
description in Latin, showing how a plant is first described and named.)
Growing 30-60cm(12-24in) high and medium-spreading 60cm(24in),
with long-petioled, evergreen leaves, with more leaflets than most (up to
five on each of the three parts); these also vary in size (5-l0 × 3-7cm/2-4 ×
1¼-3in) and they show some autumn colour. The numerous flowers are
pinkish-beige to red and pale yellow, small (up to lcm/½in) across) and are
at first borne well above the foliage. The flower stalk carries a leaf.
Cultivation – Group 2.

E. davidii Franchet, 1883.
Introduced by Martyn Rix from Sichuan, central China, in 1985, though
first collected in 1867 by the French missionary, Armand David, after
whom it is named. One of the best of all listed here for garden display
with its numerous bright yellow flowers so well carried over a long period.
Worthy of a place at the front of the border.
Height 30cm(12in) and spread 45cm(18in). Acuminate, ovate-
lanceolate leaves, coppery when young and becoming fresh green; the
leaflets measure 3-7 × 2.5-5cm (1¼-3 × 1-2in). Panicles of elegantly held
yellow, or yellow and purplish-red flowers, 2-3cm(¾-1¼in) across with

curved yellow spurs, appear from mid-spring to early summer, the flower stalks bearing a leaf. It may be less hardy than most.
Cultivation – Group 1.

E. diphyllum Graham, 1835.
From southern Japan, it was introduced about 1830.

Height 25cm(10in) and spread 30cm(12in). More or less evergreen, unusual in having only two leaflets per leaf. These are broadly oval, about 2.5-5cm(1-2in) × 1-5cm(½-2in), cordate and with a few spines. Spurless, white, pendant small flowers (1cm/½in across) are carried on stems bearing one leaf.
Cultivation – Group 1.

E. dolichostemon Stearn, 1990.
Found in Sichuan, central China, and introduced by M. Ogisu, this species was thought to be E. fargesii until named by Prof. Stearn.

Height and spread to 30cm(12in). It has evergreen basal leaves with 3 narrowly-ovate leaflets, each to 8 × 3cm(3 × 1½in). The leaflets have a pointed tip, spiny, serrated margins and a deeply cordate base. The flowering stems bear two opposite leaves and a loose inflorescence arises between them, with perhaps three dozen small flowers. Inner sepals white, spreading 9 × 3mm(⅜ × ⅛in). Petals reddish-purple; 3mm (1/8in) long, the tiny spur blunt and incurved. Conspicuous stamens protrude – the specific epithet, meaning 'long thread', refers to this.
Cultivation – Group 1.

'Enchantress'
Of garden origin – Elizabeth Strangman's fine introduction, a hybrid between E. dolichostemon and E. leptorrhizum.

Height 40cm(16in) and spread 30cm(12in). Evergreen with crinkled leaves (rather like those of E. leptorrhizum) showing considerable variability on the same plant. The three or six leaflets are relatively long and narrow, sharply pointed at the tip and cordate at their base; in some the lobes are equal, in others markedly unequal. They are a dark green and glossy above, glabrous and almost glaucous beneath, with brownish shading (especially along the main veins) which appears more pinkish-mauve beneath. They have conspicuous veins and a bristly margin. The leaflets vary in size, 8 × 3.5 to 15 × 6cm(3 × 1½ to 6 × 2½in), some leaves having only the smaller and some the larger leaflets. The latter are more glossy, more marked with brown and their smaller veins are less conspicuous. The smaller leaflets are less glossy, have more variable basal lobes and have more, and more conspicuous veins in their network between the three main veins. The small-spurred flowers (about 3-3.5cm/1¼-1½in across) are a unique shade of pale lilac-pink, shading to white at the spur tips. The flower stalks have one or two leaves: when two, the inflorescence arises from between them.
Cultivation – Group 1, preferably.

E. grandiflorum C.F.A. Morren, 1834. AGM. (*E. macranthum*, C.F.A. Morren and Decaisne, 1834)
From Japan, it was introduced into Britain around 1836. The Japanese name, *ikari-sô*, translates as 'anchor plant' and refers to the four long spurs of the flower suggesting the four-clawed anchors of their fishing boats.

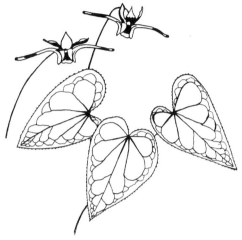

Epimedium grandiflorum

The name *E. grandiflorum*, published September 1834, has priority over the name *E. macranthum* published three months later. Both refer to the same plant introduced by C.F. von Siebold from Japan and cultivated at Ghent. Robert Marnock, first curator of the Sheffield Botanical Garden (1834-40), edited the Sheffield printed *Floricultural Magazine* and in September 1838, under 'Notices of New Plants', he wrote: '*Epimedium macranthum*, large-flowered barren-woort, ... a hardy alpine of great merit ... at Chatsworth ... last May, where it bloomed, after having endured with impunity our last severe winter out of doors.'

Height 20-30cm(8-12in) and spread 30om(12in). Bi- or tri-ternate leaves and cordate, ovate leaflets, 3-6 × 1.5-4cm(1¼-2½ × ½-2in). These are bronze-flushed when young, with spiny margins, and they usually colour well in autumn. White and rose-purple flowers, 2.5-4.5cm(1-1¾in) across, with outstretched spurs, 1-2cm(½-¾in) long. The flower stalks bear a leaf.

Cultivation – Group 1, they do not like alkaline soils.

There are several named selections (of garden origin, unless stated):

'Crimson Beauty'
It has coppery markings on the young leaves and crimson-rose flowers.

This is a doubtful name (see 'Rose Queen' below). In Professor Stearn's view 'Crimson Beauty' is the original 'Rose Queen'; Robin

White and Elizabeth Strangman agree – the Washfield list changed the name from 'Crimson Beauty' to 'Rose Queen'.

'Elfenkönigin'
Has creamy-white flowers (see 'Lilafee').

E. g. var. *hypoglaucum* Nakai ex Maekawa, 1932.
See *E. sempervirens* (page 44). It is similar to *grandiflorum* but evergreen. It has white flowers.

E. g. subsp. *koreanum* Kitamura, 1962. (*E. g.* forma *flavescens*)
From Korea and Japan, it has pale yellow flowers.

'Lilafee' ('Lilac Fairy')
With purple-tinted young growth and violet, purple and white flowers. 'Elfenkönigin' and 'Lilafee' are German cultivars introduced by Ernst Pagels, growing to 20-30cm(8-12in).

'Nanum' AGM
This is a dwarf cultivar with white flowers to 12cm(5in) and about half the size of the species. Like 'Lilafee' it is later into growth than most, and the first leaves keep low; those following the flowers are edged with red and taller (to 22cm/10in).

'Rose Queen' AGM
It has dark bronze-purple young leaves and deep rose-pink flowers with long, white-tipped spurs.

There are questions about 'Crimson Beauty' (see above) and 'Rose Queen': Robin White tells me that in Professor Stearn's view 'Crimson Beauty' is the original 'Rose Queen'. He and Elizabeth Strangman agree – the Washfield list changed the name from 'Crimson Beauty' to 'Rose Queen', calling it the 'best and brightest of the named forms of *grandiflorum* with crimson-rose flowers'. In that case what is the 'Rose Queen' of commerce? Plants previously named 'Rose Queen' at Washfield nursery are labelled 'rose form' and Professor Stearn suggests the recent 'Rose Queen' be renamed 'Rose Beauty'.

E. g. forma *violaceum* ('Violaceum')
It has purple and white flowers. Robert Marnock (see above) wrote in a 1838 issue of *Floricultural Magazine* of the 'several new species belonging to this very graceful and beautiful genus, [that] have been recently brought to this country from China. The pretty little plant [*E. violaceum*], as the name implies, has light purple or violet coloured flowers with small heart-shaped foliage. It is supposed to be hardy but this is not fully ascertained; it succeeds well when grown in the greenhouse, in a light loamy soil.'

'White Queen' AGM
Shown at the RHS on 2 May, 1967 by Miss Davenport-Jones, it has sparkling white flowers, some of the largest of the group.

E. leptorrhizum Stearn, 1933.

Introduced by Ogisu from Sichuan, China. It was described by Stearn in 1933 but has only recently become available.

Slowly spreading to make a close clump, 45cm(18in) wide by 12-24cm(5-10in) high, an evergreen with leathery, tri-foliate, spiny-margined leaves, which are, I think, among the most attractive of all epimedium leaves. The conspicuously veined, almost crinkly leaflets measure 7-11 × 3-5.5cm(3-5 × 1¼-2¼in), are ovate-lanceolate, cordate at the base and have a long pointed tip. They are bronze-brown when young, with red hairs beneath, especially along the veins, where they persist as the leaves become glaucous underneath. Large (to 4cm/1½in across) white flowers, suffused rose-lilac, with spurs 2cm(¾in) long, are borne into early summer, on a flower stalk with a leaf.

Cultivation – Group 1.

The flowers of *E.* × *perralchicum* 'Wisley' (see page 32)

E. × *perralchicum* Stearn, 1938. AGM. (*E. perralderianum* × *E. pinnatum* subsp. *colchicum*).

Of garden origin (Wisley). A robust hybrid, gradually spreading to 75cm(30in) or more in time, it grows to 40cm(16in) high. With evergreen, shining, leathery leaves with spiny margins and, often, overlapping lobes at the cordate base. The leaflets are about 6-9 × 4-8cm (2½-3½ × 1½-3in). Bright yellow flowers up to 2cm(¾in) across, with very short brown spurs. The flowers of these plants show well above the foliage for some time, before leaf growth tends to cover them. No leaf on the stalk.

Cultivation – Group 2.

'Frohnleiten'

A German cultivar, selected by Heinz Klose, it has a more toothed margin to its more elongated lealets and the largest flowers of this group, up to 2.5cm(1in) across.

'Wisley'
Height and spread to 60cm(24in), it is a selected form of the original hybrid, with large flowers (see overleaf), to 2cm/¾in, and the brightest evergreen foliage. It has less coppery markings in spring and perhaps doesn't colour quite as much as 'Frohnleiten' does in autumn.

E. perralderianum Cosson, 1862.
From Algeria; introduced to Britain about 1867. Gently spreading rhizomes make a bold, dense clump (height 30cm/12in and spread 75cm/30in or more in time). Ovate, evergreen leaflets (5-8 × 4-6cm/2-3 × 1½-2½in) are glossy and conspicuously toothed. Flowers bright yellow, up to 2cm(¾in) across, with short brown spurs, on stalks without a leaf, and well above the leaves.
Cultivation – Group 2.

E. pinnatum Fischer ex de Candolle, 1821. (*E. pinnatum* subsp. *pinnatum*; *E. pinnatum* subsp. *originarium*)
From Azerbaijan, northern Iran, it was introduced to Britain about 1849.
    Gently spreading to make evergreen clumps (height 40cm/16in and spread 75cm/30in) with ovate, cordate leathery leaflets (5-10 × 5-7cm/2-4 × 2-3in) with spiny margins. Bright yellow flowers to 2cm(¾in) across, with small brownish-purple spurs, into early summer. The flowers stand up well above the leaves: their stems, without leaves, are about 60cm(24in) tall so showing off the flowers better than most.
    Cultivation – Group 2.

E. p. subsp. colchicum (Boissier) Busch, 1903 AGM
(*E. p.* 'Elegans')
The form most usually cultivated, is from north-east Turkey to the Caucasus and was introduced about 1842. It has more rounded, less prickly leaflets, 6-13 × 4.5-9cm/2½-5 × 1¼-3½in and makes a dense clump with its short rhizomes (height 30-40cm/12-16in and spread 50cm/20in, slowly increasing). Yellow flowers, with brown or yellow spurs, held well above the leaves. Has been a parent for *E.* × *perralchicum*, *E.* × *versicolor* and *E.* × *warleyense*.

E. pubigerum (de Candolle) C.F.A. Morren and Decaisne, 1834.
From the southern shores of the Black Sea – Bulgaria, Turkey and into west Georgia – it was introduced into Britain in 1887 by Ellen Willmott from a garden in Geneva.
    Evergreen, height and spread 45cm(18in), distinctly glossy leaves, its leaflets (up to nine, in 3s) more rounded than most and 4-8 × 3.5-6cm (1½-3 × 1½-2½in). Creamy-white or yellowish-white flowers (some-

times inner sepals pale pink), and small (to 1cm/½in across), are at first borne well above the foliage. Flower stalks with one leaf.

Cultivation – Group 2.

E. × rubrum C.F.A. Morren 1854. AGM. (*E. alpinum* × *E. grandiflorum*). Of garden origin, it has been known in Britain since about 1854 (see page 23). Different forms exist as the cross apparently has occurred in more than one place (see page 23).

Slowly spreading (height and spread 30-45cm/12-24in), its divided leaves, strikingly and beautifully red-flushed when young, turn red and reddish-brown in autumn and usually remain remarkably good through the winter – it is a pity to cut them off! Leaflets 6-10 × 3.5-7cm/2½-4 × 1½-3in. Crimson and pale yellow flowers, 2cm(¾in) across, with short spurs, on stems with a leaf.

Cultivation – preferably Group 1 but very tolerant of 2.

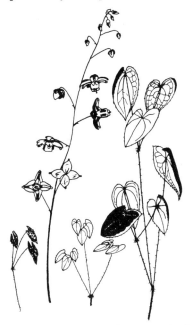

Epimedium × *versicolor* **'Sulphureum'** (see overleaf)

E. × versicolor C.F.A. Morren, 1849. (*E. grandiflorum* × *E. pinnatum* subsp. *colchicum*)

Of garden origin: 'Sulphureum' and 'Versicolor' (see below) are among the first hybrids deliberately made, by crossing the parents at the Ghent Botanic Garden over 150 years ago.

Height and spread 40cm/16in. Biternate, evergreen leaves and cordate, ovate leaflets, 5-9cm/2-3½in × 5-7cm/2-3in. Young foliage is often strikingly coloured in shades of copper-red and brown. Small (0.5-2cm/½-¾in across), pink and yellow flowers, with short reddish spurs, are borne on stems which may or may not carry a leaf.

'Cupreum' C.F.A. Morren, 1849.
It has copper-red flowers and somewhat less persistent foliage.

'Sulphureum' (C.F.A. Morren) Stearn, 1934. AGM.
See 'Neosulphureum' below (and overleaf).

'Neosulphureum' Stearn, 1938.
These two cultivars are very difficult to separate at a glance. The most consistent difference is in the base of the leaflet with a wide open sinus in 'Neosulphureum'. This has pale yellow flowers and the young foliage has its coppery colour more diffused across the leaves than does 'Sulphureum', where it tends to be in patches. 'Sulphureum' has, perhaps, slightly darker yellow flowers with slightly longer spurs and sometimes more leaflets per leaf. With me, it also spreads more widely, making patches 1.5m(4½ft) or more across and is probably the strongest growing of all epimediums.

'Versicolor' Stearn, 1934.
It has a particularly good coppery-red young foliage and it colours again in autumn before dying in winter. Gently creeping, it has rose-pink sepals and yellow petals.
    Cultivation – Groups 1 or 2.

E. × warleyense Stearn, 1938. (*E. alpinum* × *E. pinnatum* subsp. *colchicum*)
From Miss Willmott's once famous but now derelict garden, Warley Place, near Brentwood, Essex. Sue Hough, of the Hampshire HPS Group, and a great enthusiast of Ellen Willmott and her plants, tells me that when Professor Stearn was working on his monograph in 1932 he received this hybrid from Miss Willmott, as *E. perralderianum*. Miss Willmott was said to have been thinking of writing on *Epimedium* before the First World War and this was one of the plants she had grown for that purpose. It dates from about 1909. Stearn named the plant in 1938 and it became generally available. A German reference, Hansen and Stahl, gives it as 'Ellen Willmott', which is sensible as there is now another cultivar (see below).
    Spreading to 75cm(30in) and growing to a height of 50cm(20in) or more, patch-forming, with ovate, evergreen, divided leaves which are red-tinted in spring and autumn. The leaflets are 7.5-12 × 4.5-9cm(3-5 × 1¾-3½in) and sparsely spiny. Flowers are flattish, about 1.5-2cm(¾in) across. The inner sepals are reddish-orange, with darker orange lines; the very small spurred yellow petals are shaded brown near their tips and the

spur held close to the sepals. The flower stems may or may not bear a leaf.

'Orangekönigin' Pagels
This recent cultivar, raised/introduced by Ernst Pagels, seems to spread less quickly to make a denser clump and has paler, slightly less red and slightly more orange flowers, which appear a little earlier.
Cultivation – Groups 1 or 2.

E. × youngianum Fischer and Meyer, 1846. (*E. diphyllum* × *E. grandiflorum*)
May have originated in the wild in Japan, or garden origin (see overleaf).

Generally this group makes smaller plants than any of the others, growing to a height of 20-30cm(8-12in) and spreading to 30cm(12in). Thin, wavy-edged, almost spineless leaves divide into spear-shaped leaflets with one lobe distinctly larger, borne on red-tinted petioles and with a varying number (two, six, seven or nine) of leaflets, 2-8 × 1-5cm(¾-3 × ½-2in). Variable flowers, showing their hybrid origin: some with spurs, some without, and white, lilac or pale rose coloured. The flower stems bear a leaf.

Cultivation – Group 1 and preferring a little more moisture than most.

'Merlin' A. Doncaster
Introduced by Washfield Nursery, it is larger and more persistent in leaf than other × *youngianum* cultivars, has purple-flushed young growth and small-spurred, dusky mauve flowers 2cm(¾in) across.

'Niveum' (Vilmorin-Andrieux) Stearn, 1934. AGM.
It has small (to 1cm/½in across) flowers, pure white, some spurred and some not, and often very colourful young foliage – height 20cm(8in) and spread 24cm(10in).

'Roseum' (Vilmorin-Andrieux) Stearn, 1934.
It has variable foliage and dusky pink to different shades of purple flowers (*The RHS Plant Finder* equates 'Lilacinum' with this).

Epimedium × youngianum (pages 35-36)

A Few Lists

FLOWERING TIMES

(1995 – probably rather an early year)

Early (over by end April): *EE.* 'Frohnleiten', *grandiflorum* forms, × *rubrum*, × *warleyense*, 'Orangekönigin', 'Wisley'.

Mid (over by mid-to-end of May): *EE. alpinum*, × *cantabrigiense*, *diphyllum*, × *versicolor* 'Sulphureum', × *v.* 'Neosulphureum', × *youngianum* cultivars.

Late: *EE. grandiflorum* 'Nanum', 'Lilafee'

In 1996, none had come into flower by the middle of April, when some of those in the early group above produced flowers.

MY FAVOURITE TWELVE (... SO FAR!)

EE. acuminatum, davidii, 'Enchantress', *grandiflorum* 'Nanum', *g.* 'Rose Queen', *g.* 'White Queen', *leptorrhizum*, × *perralchicum* 'Wisley', × *rubrum*, × *youngianum* 'Merlin', × *y.* 'Niveum', × *versicolor* 'Sulphureum'.

BEGINNER'S BEST FIVE

(for ease of culture and freedom from problems)

EE. 'Enchantress', × *perralchicum* 'Wisley', *perralderianum*, × *rubrum*, × *versicolor* 'Sulphureum'. If you could grow only one, probably *E.* × *versicolor* 'Sulphureum' is a good choice, especially if you want ground cover.

DECIDUOUS

EE. alpinum, davidii, grandiflorum and its forms, × *youngianum* and its forms.

FOR GOOD WINTER COLOUR

For green leaves: *EE.* × *cantabrigiense, leptorrhizum*, × *perralchicum* and its forms (especially 'Wisley'), *perralderianum, pinnatum* subsp. *colchicum*.
For russet colours: *EE.* × *rubrum*, × *versicolor* 'Neosulphureum' and × *v.* 'Sulphureum' and, to a lesser extent, × *warleyense*.

Uses of *Epimedium* and *Vancouveria*

WITH THEIR EASE OF CULTURE, freedom from problems and small dimensions, these plants have many uses in our gardens. Farrer writes in *The English Rock Garden* (though obviously unaware of the variety available today): 'The barren-worts are all much of a muchness, except in the colour of their flower-flights – plants of extreme but unappreciated value for quiet shady corners of the rock garden, where they will form wide masses in time, and send up in spring and early summer 10-inch showers, most graceful and lovely, of flowers that suggest a flight of wee and monstrous columbines of waxy texture ... Then begining later than these, appear the leaves, hardly less beautiful an adornment to summer than the blossoms to spring. For these are of a delicious green, much divided into pointed leaflets, and borne on wiry stems ... you may rely upon [*Epimedium*] being of the easiest and most indestructible temper in any cool place, ... and of the most astonishing and delicate loveliness alike in form and in colour of its dainty crystalline flowers in spring.' Today, our rock gardens are probably too small to accommodate many epimediums but they have many uses elsewhere.

GROUND COVER

Their relatively thick cover of leaves and entangling rhizomes keep down weeds. The evergreen forms last through the winter. Whether green or coloured shades of brown, they remain attractive. The relatively broad leaf with its hard shiny surface reflects light so that they show up well. The delicate, wiry stems make an effective contrast. They are useful in awkward places. Though prefering moist, leaf-mould soil, they will tolerate a considerable degree of dryness under trees and between shrubs and choosing the more spreading sorts helps here. Especially useful are *EE*. × *cantabrigiense*, × *perralchicum* and its cultivars 'Frohnleiten' and 'Wisley', *perralderianum, pinnatum* subsp. *colchicum*, × *rubrum*, × *versicolor* 'Neosulphureum' and 'Sulphureum', × *warleyense* and 'Orangekönigin'. There are good examples of their use at Dartington Hall, Devon, and at Wisley, in the woodland. At Wisley they are (deliberately?) planted at strategic points such as the corners of beds, near paths, where otherwise the ground may look bare, and people be tempted to take a short cut! They also look attractive planted alongside steps and in paving. *Vancouveria hexandra* is equally effective, though the other two *Vancouveria* species are less vigorous and would not cope with difficult places nor strong competition.

BACKGROUND PLANTING

Perhaps suitable as background planting for the larger bulbs, such as daffodils and lilies, which could push up through a not too thick cover. If the epimediums were more spread out then snowdrops, erythroniums and wood anemones would survive and, of course, flower just before or as the non-evergreen sorts grow their new leaves.

As plants at the back of the border which flower and come into leaf early, giving colour before the main planting grows up and obscures them, they can be useful. The plant forms a fine mound of foliage in most of them – valuable in shape as well as in the colour of the young leaves. This does not suggest that they should only be used at the back of a bed – their mound of foliage fits them for a front place too, and I recommend especially *E. davidii* and *E. grandiflorum* 'Nanum' for this.

COMPANION PLANTING

A number of early flowering plants from similar woodland conditions fit well with epimediums and other herbaceous berberids – hellebores, most hostas, bergenias, dicentras, some geraniums, polygonatums, pulmonarias, uvularias and smilacinas etc. as well as many ferns. A splendid spring bed could be made with epimediums (perhaps best with the 'clumpers' rather than the 'spreaders' in most gardens) and the above, giving contrasts in height, foliage colour and texture. To make it an all-the-year-round bed, they could be followed by geraniums and lilies. Japanese anemones, *Tricyrtis* and the colouring foliage of some *Hosta, Epimedium, Uvularia*, would continue to provide colour in autumn, still leaving evergreen ferns, bergenias, pulmonarias and epimediums with the early bulbs. And, as well as their varied foliage, most will have flowers in their season too! Some of the epimediums more tolerant of sunnier spots could accompany those hostas and bergenias which grow well in such situations.

ECOLOGICAL PLANTING

Epimediums are useful plants for the 'ecological' or 'natural' planting now being much lauded. It seems to me to be an adaptation or extension of William Robinson's style and Gertrude Jekyll's planting in drifts method, though perhaps using more 'wild' plants. Both, however, require more space than is possible in many of today's gardens but in public gardens seeking low-maintenance it is a very good way to use plants (if the public disapproval of the inevitable 'untidiness' can be overcome). Most epimediums could stand their ground against the larger plants and cover the ground pleasingly. I first saw an example of this at the International Garden Exhibition at Munich in 1983 and, though I cannot remember seeing many epimediums (I was most impressed by their use of grasses and *Hemerocallis*), they would have fitted in very well. Herr Klaus Kaiser, author of a book on anemones and a German landscape architect, tells me that epimediums are very important for the German way of using perennials in *lebensbereiche* or 'ecological planting'. There is a similar range of *Epimedium* available in Germany to that in Britain and they are quite widely used.

FLOWERS

Although most could not perhaps be described as showy, epimedium flowers give pleasure and intrigue by their unusual shapes. (Some, like *E. acuminatum* and *E. leptorrhizum* could possibly be planted raised up to eye-level where it would be easier to see their hanging, downward-facing flowers). Flowers and foliage are useful to flower arrangers, especially in late spring and early summer when not much other herbaceous foliage is available, and the leaves dry successfully.

POTS

Though not often used in pots and containers, epimediums will grow well in them. Of course, watering has to be watched in summer and low temperatures in winter – when it would perhaps be best to sink the pots in sand, leaf mould or in the soil to avoid freezing. This is is especially true of the Chinese species; these could probably be used for early flowering in a cold or slightly heated greenhouse and, if they looked like Robin White's display at the RHS, would be splendid. I haven't grown any in this way but I have kept several kinds in pots very successfully.

THE ROCK GARDEN

Though most kinds are probably too large, some could be useful for shady places in a rock garden. *Epimedium × youngianum* and its cultivars, and *E. grandiflorum* 'Nanum' would be suitable.

All the other genera mentioned in this booklet are uncommon plants, not showy (except perhaps for those *Podophyllum* with their marked leaves and a well-grown *Diphylleia*) but are pleasing 'quiet' plants. They are especially suited to a woodland garden and mix well with anemones, dicentras, disporums, ferns, hostas, *Tricyrtis*, trilliums, and numerous bulbs. These combinations don't depend upon extensive woodland – they can be made under one small garden tree and a shrub or two, and will give lasting pleasure, and with careful choice, year-long colour.

New Epimediums of Recent Introduction

ROBIN WHITE

ALTHOUGH CHINA IS HOME TO MOST EPIMEDIUMS and such decorative species as *E. acuminatum* and *E. davidii* were discovered in the mid-nineteenth century, only one Chinese species (*E. sagittatum*) was in cultivation in the West by the 1930s. It is only since the early 1980s that the Chinese species previously known only as herbariun specimens, as well as many new species, have been introduced into cultivation.

At present, the genus comprises 46 species, in contrast to the 21 recognised in 1938, when Professor W.T. Stearn published his monograph *Epimedium and Vancouveria*. Although now an octogenarian, he is working on a revision, which should he published in 1997. Professor Stearn is responsible for identifying and naming many of the species recently discovered in China.

It is important to stress that new forms, species and natural hybrids are still being discovered in China. The mountainous, wooded terrain of the country where they are found makes it possible for different species to be isolated in valleys only a few miles apart. It is also possible that new species are still in the process of evolving. The exact identification of several specimens collected has yet to be decided.

Considerable difficulties have been experienced in trying to find the type localities of species collected by some of the Victorian plant hunters e.g. *E. fargesii*, *E. platypetalum* and *E. sutchuenense*. The early botanists often employed local people to collect for them and the diversity of spellings in which European collectors rendered local Chinese names are two obvious reasons for this. Western gardeners have Mikinori Ogisu to thank for most of the recent introductions to cultivation. A Japanese botanist who has been working on the flora of Sichuan for fifteen years, his perseverance and generosity have recently been recognised by the RHS with the award in 1995 of the Veitch Memorial Medal.

The worth of most of these recent introductions has yet to be evaluated under garden conditions. However, most of them will be as hardy as those already grown, will tolerate alkaline soils, have evergreen foliage, and carry their flowers above new leaves. These are all garden worthy points which, together with large flower size or large numbers of flowers per inflorescence, show great promise for the future.

RECENTLY INTRODUCED SPECIES

(NB. Figures given are collector's numbers e.g. Og. 82.010 = Ogisu is the collector, 82. = 1982 and 010 the site.)

E. brevicornu Maximowicz
Named in 1890. A very hardy species, in which the fresh young foliage gives the impression of a maidenhair fern.

The two stem leaves on the flowering stem consist of nine ovate, or broadly ovate, leaflets. Foliage deciduous; golden autumn colour. New young foliage may be plain, pale green (Ogisu 82.010) or with large purple patches (Og. 88.010). Rhizome compact. Inner sepals lcm(½in) long, white, much longer than the petals.

E. campanulatum Ogisu. Og. 93.087
Discovered by Mikinori Ogisu in Sichuan and named by him (*Kew Bulletin*, May, 1996).

Foliage evergreen. Rhizome campact or spreading – but not very far. Inflorescence compound, 7-21cm.(3-8in) high, many flowered. Flowers cup-shaped, pendulous. Petals spurless, pale sulphur yellow. Inner sepals pale sulphur yellow or red-tinged.

E. dolichostemon Stearn. Og. 81.011
Named by Professor Stearn in 1990.

Plant in flower about 30cm(12in) high. Evergreen foliage, young foliage splashed crimson – veins flushed crimson in winter. Rhizome spreading – but not very far. Large, compound inflorescence. Inner sepals elliptic, white, 8-9 × 0.25cm(³/8 × ¹/8in). Petals 0.3cm(¹/8in), reddish-purple, strongly incurved. Conspicuous, yellowish-green stamens. Another collection (Og. 81.010) has distinctly narrower, more attractive foliage.

This species is available commercially in the UK. Its tall many flowered inflorescence, held well above the foliage, makes it a good garden plant and a good parent for hybridising. Hybrids between it and *E. acuminatum* have been raised in Japan, one of which, *E. kaguyahime*, is now also available in the UK (see below).

E. ecalcaratum G.Y. Zhong
A new species, named in 1991, it is a calcicole but may prove to be less hardy than most. The abundance of dainty flowers produced in spring will, I think, appeal to alpine house and conservatory owners.

Evergreen foliage, strongly flushed purple in winter. Rhizome long-creeping. Flowers yellow, bell-shaped and, in the clone Og. 93.082, without spurs (plants with spurred flowers have been observed in the wild).

E. fargesii Franchet

Named in 1894 but until recently known only from the type specimen. This species has yet to be trialled in the open but under cold glass the exceptional beauty of the flowers are sure to win many admirers.

Foliage evergreen. The leaflets are very attractive, being long and narrow with conspicuous spined edges. Young foliage is crimson blotched. Rhizome compact. Flowering height 20-40cm(8-16in). Inflorescence compound or simple. Inner sepals are long (1.5-2cm/¾in) and narrow and soon reflex. Petals are much shorter than inner sepals, dark purple, spur-shaped. Long, conspicuously protruding stamens. Og. 93.023 has pink inner sepals while Og. 93.053 has white.

E. flavum Stearn. Og. 92.036

Named in 1994 by Professor Stearn, this species is similar to *E. davidii*, but has much larger, pale yellow inner sepals. No trials in the open yet. Pot-grown plants have produced large quantities of flowers in a single flush of great beauty.

Foliage evergreen. Rhizome compact. Early flowering – flowering height about 30cm(12in). Inflorescence simple, with 3-10 flowers. Flowers about 3cm/1¼in across, bright lemon in colour. Inner sepals 1 × 0.5cm(8 × ⅛in). Petals with elongated spur 1.5cm(⅝in) long, expanded at base into a large lamina.

E. franchetii Stearn. Og. 87.001

The clone has been given the cultivar name 'Brimstone Butterfly' by Prof. Stearn (*Kew Bulletin*, May 1996). This very handsome species was thought for some time after collection to be a yellow form of *E. acuminatum*.

Foliage evergreen. Leaflets large, up to 14cm(5½in) long, pinkish-bronze when young, ageing to glossy green. Rhizome compact. Inflorescence simple, many-flowered (14-25). Flowers large (4.5cm/1¾in across) with pale greenish-yellow inner sepals. Petals much longer than inner sepals, pale sulphur yellow; spur without lamina.

E. latisepalum Stearn. Og. 91.002

Named by Professor Stearn in 1993. Under good conditions of cultivation, this species produces the largest flowers I have seen, though it has not been trialled in the open yet.

Foliage evergreen. Rhizome long-creeping. Early flowering with flowering stems up to 30cm(12in) but leaning in habit, rather than erect. Inflorescence simple or compound with few (6-10) flowers. Flowers large, 4-5cm/1½-2in across. Inner sepals elliptic, 1.5 × 1cm(⅝ × ⅜in) long, pale cream in colour, with faint pink veins. Petals much larger than inner sepals, white with yellow or purple tinge at their base. They are expanded into a lamina at their base.

E. *membranaceum* K. Meyer

Known since 1922, plants were introduced by Martyn Rix in the early 1970s but unfortunately were sold as *E. elongatum*. This species is one of the latest to flower (late May onwards) and flowers are produced for a long period in succession provided the plant is kept moist. This may be one of the few Chinese species to object to lime in the soil.

Foliage is evergreen, with a compact rhizome. Flowering stems are tall, 50-60cm(20-24in). Inflorescence compound. Flowers 3-5cm(1¼-2in) across, pale yellow. Inner sepals 0.5 × 0.25cm(¼ × ⅛in). Petals much longer than inner sepals, horn shaped, with no lamina at the base, 1.5-2.5cm(¾-1in) long.

E. *ogisui* Stearn. Og. 91.001

Named in 1993 by Professor Stearn after its collector. This beautiful species is wonderful as a pot-grown specimen but may prove less successful in the garden, due to its horizontal flower stems – it was discovered growing on shady cliffs near a waterfall.

Foliage evergreen, orange/bronze flushed when young, dark green on the upper surface, silvery on the lower. Rhizome slender, long-creeping. Flower stems almost horizontal. Inflorescence simple, few flowered. Flowers large, about 2.5cm(1in) across. Inner sepals white, 1.5-2 × 0.7-1cm(¾ × ¼-⅜in). Petals similar length to inner sepals, white, expanded at base into a lamina.

E. *pauciflorum* K.C. Yen (*E. platypetalum* var. *tenue*)

A new species named in 1994. A low growing species, 10-15cm(4-6in), yet to be assessed in the garden but may be useful as ground cover.

Foliage evergreen. Rhizome very thin 1-2mm(¹/16in), long-creeping, much branched. Inflorescence simple, few-flowered. Flowers large, 2-2.5cm(¾-1in) across. Inner sepals pale lilac pink, 1 × 0.25cm(½ × ⅛in). Petals longer than inner sepals, white – tinged pink, expanded into three laminae at their base.

E. *platypetalum* K. Meyer. Og. 93.085

Named in 1922, this species is unlikely to prove hardy.

Foliage evergreen or semi-evergreen, mottled purple in low temperatures. Leaflets characteristically almost circular. Rhizome slender (1-2mm/¹/16in) and long-creeping. Small campanulate flowers, yellow and spurless.

E. *pubescens* Maximowicz, 1877.

Known since the late nineteenth-century, this tall species (up to 60cm/24in) is widespread in China. Although the individual flowers are small, their abundance gives a charming effect. The young foliage of Ogisu 91.003 is very handsomely mottled with crimson. This is one of the earliest species into growth and flower and so needs careful siting to avoid frost damage.

Inflorescence compound, flowers 1cm(½in) across. Inner sepals white, 0.5 × 0.15cm(¼ × ¹/₁₆in) across. Petals shorter than inner sepals, golden brown.

E. sempervirens Nakai ex Maekawa

Named in 1932, this species agrees with *E. grandiflorum* in almost everything except its evergreen foliage. Some botanists have classed it as a subspecies of *E. grandiflorum* – it has been known as *E. grandiflorum* var. *hypoglaucum* – but it is retained as a species by modern Japanese botanists.

This species is likely to be intolerant of alkaline soils. Typically, the flowers are creamy-white but I have two different colour forms:

'Aurora' with lavender flowers

'Candy Hearts' with silvery pink flowers and pinkish young foliage, evolving to a rose border to the new leaves.

E. stellulatum 'Wudang Star' L 1193

Collected in 1983 by Roy Lancaster, growing in cracks in limestone rocks at Wudang Shan, Hubei, central China. Identified as a new species and named by Prof. Stearn in 1992.

Foliage evergreen, leaf veins flushed dark crimson in cold weather. Rhizome short-creeping. Flower stems 20-35cm(8-14in) high. Inflorescence compound, bearing up to 40 flowers. Inner sepals white, 1.25 × 0.25cm(⁹/₁₆ × ¹/₈in). Petals shorter than inner sepals, orange-brown, with slight lamina and blunt nectariferous spur.

E. wushanense T.S. Ying

Named in 1975, this wonderful foliage plant may not prove to be hardy throughout the UK.

Foliage evergreen, mottled dull purple when young. Exceptionally long, narrow leaflets (9-23 × 1.8-4.5cm/3½-9 × ⁷/₈-1¼in). The spines on the edge of the leaflets are strong and sharp enough to pierce human skin. Rhizome spreading – but not very far. Inflorescence compound, 50-80cm(20-32in) high. Flowers 3.5cm(1½in) across, in the typical form they are pale yellow but Og. 92.009 has buff-pink, suffused purple at the base. Inner sepals broadly elliptic, 1.25-1.5cm(⁹/₁₆-¾in). Petals spur-shaped, 1.5-2cm(to ¾in), without lamina at base.

RECENTLY INTRODUCED HYBRIDS

'Amanogowa' (*E. dolichostemon* × *E. acuminatum*)
A hybrid of garden origin from Japan.

Foliage evergreen, mottled when young. Rhizome compact. Height of flowering stem 30-60cm(12-24in). Each stem carries several dozen flowers with broad white inner sepals and bronze spur-shaped petals, shorter than the inner sepals.

'Kaguyahime' (*E. acuminatum* × *E. dolichostemon*)
An exceptionally beautiful hybrid from the garden of Mr Yamaguchi in Japan.

Foliage evergreen, flushed pink-bronze in winter. Rhizome compact. Many-flowered compound inflorescence, 30-60cm(12-24in) in height. Broad inner sepals are pink, and the spur-shaped petals, shorter than the inner sepals, are purple.

E. × *omeiense* Stearn ('Emei Shan') Og. 82.001
A natural hybrid between *E. acuminatum* and *E. fangii*, found on Emei Shan.

Foliage evergreen. Rhizome compact. Inflorescence compound, 40-60cm(16-24in) in height. Flowers large, 4-5cm(1½-2in) across. Inner sepals dull rose. Petals much longer than inner sepals, with a strongly curved spur, yellow, suffused with red streaks.

E. × *omeiense* 'Stormcloud' Og. 82.002
A selection from the same hybrid swarm as Og. 82.001 i.e. from *E. fangii* × *E. acuminatum*.

Foliage evergreen. Rhizome short – creeping. Tall (50-60cm/22-24in) compound inflorescence. A notable feature of this hybrid is the variable size and shape of the inner sepals, often on the same flower. They vary in shape from a broad dome to a spur. Petals are much longer than the inner sepals, with a strongly curved spur. Flower colour is a sombre purple-bronze.

References

(The plant names in brackets towards the end of entries are the new taxa described.)

P.P.H. But, S.Y. Hu & Y.C. King (1980). Vascular Plants Used In Chinese Medicine. *Fitoterapia*, 51, 5.

Duke, J.A. & Wain, K.K. (1981). *Medicinal Plants of the World.* (Computer Index).

Duke, J.A. & Ayensu, E.S. (1985). *Medicinal Plants of China.* 2 vols. Reference Publications, Algonah, Michigan.

Hansen, K. & Stahl, F. (1990). *Die Stauden und ihre Lebensbereiche.* Stuttgart.(Transl. by Tina Wasmeier).

Hartwell, J.L. (1967-71). Plants Used Against Cancer. A Survey, *Lloydia*, 30-34. Quarterman Publications Inc., Lawrence, Mass.

Jelitto, L. & Schacht, W. (1990). 3rd ed. Schacht, W. & Fessler, A. *Hardy Herbaceous Perennials.* Timber Press: Portland, Oregon.

Keys, J.D. (1976). *Chinese Herbs, Their Botany, Chemistry and Pharmacodynamics.*

Loconte, H. (1993). *Berberidaceae.* In Kubitzki, (Ed.) *Families and Genera of Vascular Plants*, 2, 147-152. Springer Verlag, Berlin.

Meacham, C.A. (1980). Phylogeny of the *Berberidaceae*, with an evaluation of classifications. *Systematic Botany*, 5, 148-172.

Phillips, R. & Rix, M. (1991). *Perennials* (Vol.1) Pan Books: London.

Reid, D.P. (1993). *Chinese Herbal Medicine.* C.F.W. Publications, Hong Kong.

Rix, M. & Phillips R. (1981). *The Bulb Book.* Pan Books, London.

Rix, M. (1982). *The Plantsman*, 4, Pt. 1. June.

Stearn, W.T. (1933). Some Chinese species of *Epimedium. J. of Bot. London*, 71. (*E. leptorrhizum*).

Stearn, W.T. (1938). *Epimedium* and *Vancouveria*, a Monograph. *Journal of the Linnean Society, Botany*, 51, 409-535. (*EE. macrosepalum, × perralchicum, × warleyense*). Until now the only detailed botanical account but his new monograph, to be published in 1997, will supersede it.

Stearn, W.T. (1979). A new hybrid *Epimedium* (*E. × cantabrigiense*). *The Plantsman*, 1.

Stearn, W.T. (1989). *Epimedium* and *Vancouveria. European Garden Flora*, 3.

Stearn W.T. (1990). *Epimedium dolichostemon* (*Berberidaceae*) and other Chinese species of *Epimedium. Kew Bull.*, 45. (*E. dolichostemon*).

Stearn, W.T. (1993). New large-flowered Chinese species of *Epimedium* (*Berberidaceae*). *Kew Mag.*, 10. (*EE. latisepalum, ogisui*)

Stearn, W.T. (1993). The small-flowered Chinese species of *Epimedium* (*Berberidaceae*). *Kew Bull.*, 48. (*E. stellulatum*).
Stearn, W.T. (1995). New Chinese taxa of *Epimedium* (*Berberidaceae*) from Sichuan. *Curtis's Bot. Mag.*, 12. (*EE. fangii, flavum*, × *omeiense*).
Stearn, W.T. (1996). *Epimedium acuminatum* and allied Chinese species. *Kew Bull.*, 51. (*E. franchetii*).
Tang S. & Palmer, M. (1986). *Chinese Herbal Prescription*. Ryder & Co. and Century Hutchinson.
Watanabe, M. Unpublished correspondence. Japan.
Wee Yeow Chin & Hsuan Keng. (1992). *An Illustrated Dictionary of Chinese Medical Herbals*. C.R.C.S. Publications, North America.
White, R. (1995). Information Sheet on epimediums in cultivation at Blackthorn Nursery. Blackthorn Nursery.
White, R. (1996). *The Garden*, 121, 4. April. RHS, London.

NATIONAL COLLECTION HOLDERS

Mr David Barker, Stone Pine, Hyde Lane, Danbury, Chelmsford, Essex CM3 4LT. Tel: 01245.22232. Open by appt.
Mrs Margaret Owen, Acton Pigot, Acton Burnell, Shropshire. Tel: 01743.718846 or 01694.731209. Open by appt.
The Curator, RHS Garden, Wisley, Woking, Surrey GU23 6QB. Tel: 01483.224234.

Glossary

androecium - the male parts of the flower (stamens)

anther - part of the stamen which contains pollen

axil - angle between leaf stalk or smaller stem and main stem

axillary - growing from the axil

berry - a fleshy fruit, usually containing several seeds

caducous - short-lived or falling early (e.g. sepals)

calyx - outer part of the flower, usually green, made up of sepals

capsule - a dry dehiscent fruit, developing from more than one carpel and containing several seeds

carpel - a unit of the female part of the flower (gynoecium), made up of an ovary containing the ovules which become seeds, style and stigma (collectively = pistil)

compound - consisting of more than one part e.g. a leaf made up of leaflets or an inflorescence with branched stems.

cordate - heart-shaped

corolla - the petals of the flower, usually coloured

cymose - an inflorescence in which the growing point forms the flower, so that continued growth of the inflorescence is by forming new lateral growing point/s

dehiscent - splitting open of fruit along a line to shed its seeds, or anther its pollen

endemic - found only in a particular place or area

entire - leaves without lobes, edges not divided or toothed

filament - the stalk of the stamen

genus - category in classification which groups together all those species which have common characteristics e.g. *Epimedium*

glabrous - without hairs, smooth

gynoecium - the female part of the flower, made up of one or more carpels (pistils)

hermaphrodite - having both male and female reproductive organs in the same flower

hybrid - resulting from crossing two species or subspecies

hybrid swarm (swarm) - group of plants resulting from hybridisation & subsequent recrossings with the parents or between themselves, giving a continuous series of forms

inflorescence - the flowering part of the stem including flowers and bracts

lamina - blade of leaf or petal, on either side of midrib

limb (or blade) - flat part of sepal or petal the rest of which is tubular

lobe - parts of a partially divided leaf

panicle - strictly a branched racemose inflorescence, though often used for any branched inflorescence

pedicel - stalk of a single flower

peduncle - stalk of an inflorescence

peltate - leaf with its stalk attached at the centre of its underside

perianth - the outer floral parts: sepals and petals

perianth segments - the separate parts of the perianth, especially when these are not distinct

petal - one of the inner perianth parts, the coloured part of the flower, they make up the corolla

petaloid - brightly coloured, resembling petals

petiole - stalk of a leaf which joins it to a node on the stem

protandrous - stamens mature before ovaries

protogynous - ovaries mature before stamens

raceme - an unbranched racemose inflorescence the flowers of which have pedicels

racemose - inflorescence in which the growing point continues to grow; the youngest flowers are nearest the apex

rhizome - underground, horizontally growing stem lasting for more than one season

sepal - one of the outer perianth parts, usually green; make up the calyx

sepaloid - resembling sepals

simple - not divided

sinus - space between two lobes/teeth of a leaf or perianth part

species - a group of organisms with the same constant and distinct characters and which can interbreed; the basic unit of classification

spur - a hollow, usually conical, slender extension of the base of a perianth segment (often a petal); usually contains the nectaries

ternate - a compound leaf divided into three more or less equal parts (leaflets), which may themselves be similarly divided (bi- or tri-ternate)